REVOLVER

REVOLVER

Kevin Connolly

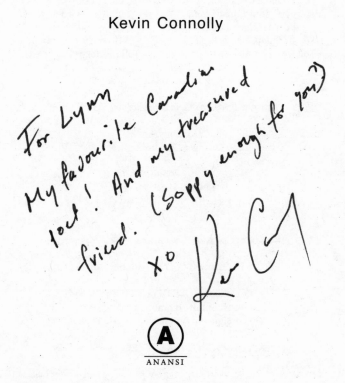

For Lynn
My favourite Canadian
poet! And my treasured
friend. (Soppy enough for you?)
xo

A

ANANSI

Published in 2008 by
House of Anansi Press Inc.
110 Spadina Avenue, Suite 801
Toronto, ON, M5V 2K4
Tel. 416-363-4343
Fax 416-363-1017
www.anansi.ca

Distributed in Canada by
HarperCollins Canada Ltd.
1995 Markham Road
Scarborough, ON, M1B 5M8
Toll free tel. 1-800-387-0117

Distributed in the United States by
Publishers Group West
1700 Fourth Street
Berkeley, CA, 94710
Toll free tel. 1-800-788-3123

12 11 10 09 08   1 2 3 4 5

Library and Archives Canada Cataloguing in Publication

Connolly, Kevin
Revolver / Kevin Connolly.

Poems.
ISBN 978-0-88784-795-0

I. Title.

PS8555.O554R48 2008   C811'.54   C2007-907085-X

Library of Congress Control Number: 2007940445

Cover design: Bill Douglas at The Bang
Cover photo: Eamon Mac Mahon
Text design and typesetting: Ingrid Paulson

 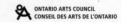

Canada Council   Conseil des Arts   ONTARIO ARTS COUNCIL
for the Arts   du Canada   CONSEIL DES ARTS DE L'ONTARIO

*We acknowledge for their financial support of our publishing program the Canada Council
for the Arts, the Ontario Arts Council, and the Government of Canada through
the Book Publishing Industry Development Program (BPIDP).*

Printed and bound in Canada

CONTENTS

V

I wish to be misunderstood;
that is,
to be understood from your perspective.
　—BILL KNOTT

I

TERRE HAUTE

We're used to a season progressing logically,
then, heading south by car, it suddenly
makes no sense in reverse: a race from
ice to snow, gray earth and nippled trees,
pooled water and mud, then the first white blades,
seeming to expire when they're really
cutting way for flowers. Dun, flat fields
—all at once, three brilliant bantam hens
over the wire, Technicolor peril beside the
interstate, its football-sized hawks.
Quarry, copse, mobile home, whole lives
spilling like a purse over the backyard.
Swamp, acres of razed cornfields waiting for seed
—experimental hybrids—which,
now you think of it, is odd, seeing as corn
really isn't much *but* seed, hundreds per stalk,
a few spare knocked off the cob would do.
Over the state line, first exit sign (you can't
find the camera): "Downer, 1 mile."
At the Flying J near Terre Haute, giants
lumber to the buffet like livestock.
They'll never make it, you think, but then
the bill comes and it's three plates each
piled up with straws and Jell-O and the ends
of fish-sticks. Velvet at the checkout preens
at the mention of her unique handle—
says she's heard of fourteen other Velvets,
but just one with her middle name:
"When the doll came out, I ran right out

and got one." Though she's not real sure
why the name didn't catch: like
Crystal or Chyna or Cheyenne.

This is both geography and biography,
feel free to jump in whenever you want...

Looked at briefly, it seems clear what this is,
where it might have come from.
Like this hammer, for example—
how to pick it up, what to do with it.
Sink a nail, of course, then use the claw
to dry your drawers, cash out a car window.
Just (exactly) like a bird, which stands for nothing
but itself, though it sometimes conjures
a pleasant noise, for some, even reminiscent
of a song, while for the bird, and for today
—the only conversation that means anything
now—it's just noise, a troubling of the air.
In such landscapes, what can you truly know
of anything: of trucking trends or travellers'
diarrhea or the grooming preferences of birds?
You read meaning into tarmac test strips, faces,
during piss breaks scanning the tabloids
filled with personal ads for "rural singles,"
or at roadside oases where you pause, bleary,
for a map or a book-on-tape or a weather warning.
For that matter, what could they really know
(if that's even a word anymore) about us,
about themselves—bright bristling rushing
surfaces, running lights and wind farms
and vanity plates. Arena rock and Golden Miles;

improv demolition derby courses next to clumsy roadside Calvarys; White Castles and giant inflatable gorillas colliding in the dark, following pioneer wagon trails and diverted creek run-offs, past towering Quonsets, light-jewelled refinery catwalks, while the graying muscle of the continent groans, turns over: constant, rolling, hopeful, unimpressed.

AUDITION PIECE

To those who drowned in history:
sorry if it was me who held you down

To those dying of real diseases, sorry,
my bad, too busy throwing up lunch

And to those who wandered into a fog
of democracy...too bad, too bad,

but if you want to create an electorate
you got to break a few legs...

And to those who stir those legs,
every hour, so they don't atrophy:

Pick up the pace babe, we're not
paying you to look pretty...

That would be our job, our *role*, for
which we're very well paid

COMPANY

Bloom says it's about erasing others,
digesting them, spitting them out as you.
Really it's more about smothering yourself,
your shaky lines, knowing in advance
they're unworthy of the next bloom,

next fool in line—to think there really are
people who think about this, All The Time.
Think about that. How small, how human,
how fraught with hatred for your best part:

one who woke this morning passably happy,
wasp that hadn't committed its stinger just yet,
thinks of its small footsteps as having less-than-
giant echoes. As if echoes could substitute for
any company—this or the worst, anytime.

LOOK ALIVE

Felt well enough through most of it,
though there are always those grim
adjustments for family—gapes
and corners, japes and giblets—
a magician's box: the one half
dark with folded legs, the other
shot through with sworded light.
What you reveal means nothing,
or at least means little later;
the odd is always there, and what
we make of it won't last the evening.

This is all sounding very much like
me all of a sudden.... Relax, shouldn't
take more than a minute of your time,
but if it does, that's you pup,
my chair is empty. No tie, no helix,
no draw to see who wins—
we mean it like we play it, like we
always knew and hid it from the others:

No such thing as progress, just a bold
dash followed by a scripted falling back
to a position where the brave can't
stumble on the obvious and the
coward has room to make his move.
You rumbled. So rest now. Run your tongue
over time's teeth, internalize the grumble.
Dodge the rhyme, send the orders back.
Climb the salt pile, nose eternity's tide.

It's half-past-two on this berg, the others
as good as sunk. So we head for the swells,
or the shoreline — no shame in that.
It's inevitable — this passion, faux drama,
dull evasion. Still, you can't help
looking, can you? But I'm done with it.
Look sideways. Look for me in traffic.
Look alive. I'm long gone.

egg—you have a beautiful skin,
it opens like a shopping mall, releases
happy bubbles or thoughtful modesties,
scouring the hills for ancient carvings

decoy—your duck looks familiar,
like a branch of the family free of all
but one leaf, the one tired signature gesture,
an awning untroubled by rain

filibuster—your name holds some
charm, like a lake reflects the disappointment
of frogs, the teeth of distant cars, but not the
groan of masticating engines

chivalry—you have a thoughtful face,
like prom night or a canned ham, but it's
a wind that won't clean the motel, no matter
the pleading, the ten bucks a room

stage fright—your terms are
acceptable, though not what you'd call fair:
shredded rigging, oil lamps piled on the
foresails, heads bobbing in the swells

PELLUCIDAR

We're lost, and by we, of course I mean me,
both of us knowing there are only two ways to go,
onward and upward, or through that great
hole in the arctic and into Rice-Burroughs' soup.
The future arcs overhead like a flashlight played
over a child's bed sheet, tied between doors
to simulate camping—pass the marshies,
celestial fires, we have GI Joes to feed!

Backtrack a little, to the cornered hardwood
oases on the carpeted stairwells, the homunculi with
rotating martial faces, the little stair-rod tiedowns.
We strung a skipping rope there and tripped April,
Dawn's favorite babysitter. Her parents never let
her come again. And what about the indoor bats?
Roy Study and his agile racket—they were

terrifying: crash-diving the stairwells—but did
they really deserve that bloody smashdown?
Those days, Steve King was my best friend, until he
boiled down a raptor's bones and beat my extinct
and endangered species drawings at the science fair.
The okapi and white tiger, reduced to tribes of dozens;
panda, fragile bamboo porn star; the passenger
pigeon, whose flocks once darkened the sun...

JUNE BUG

Consider well the proportions of things.
Let us be thankful for the fools...
naked people have little or no influence in society.
An egg cackles as if she had laid an asteroid.
Training is everything—if you don't mind,

it doesn't matter. The peach was once a
bitter almond. Clothes make the man.
You can straighten a worm, but the
crook is in him and only waiting.

It is better to be a young june bug:
daydreamer more elegantly spelled.
Age is an issue of mind over matter;
the rest is remembering about it.
When they are gone, you may still exist.

STREET LIGHT

As it's their dim watch,
spiders hang on it, half-roasted
in the haze, singed strands still
set to catch the swarming rest—
no sport in it, none whatsoever,
whatsoever crazed things catch.

Never seen anything, never
clamoured-after, never spoiled or
even spied a warm-seeming light,
never boiled-over, reached for a
chill they'll never know.

Later…damp and drowsy…
paper serpents half-reaching,
wet-wakened, put to rest,
branches stirring, reeling out
the grim revival—Lazarus
lumbering, reeking resurrection.

Given space, even shadows rejoice,
conjoin, dissemble and conjure.
Some nights you can be lost
among leaves, among spiders,
shadows yearning to be leaves,
that little step past sleep.

IN A WAY,

canal is an improvement on *river*
and thought precludes effective action
in a way too complicated to acknowledge
bright birds are airborne messages, in the
way a fountain knows its square, a cactus
is a low-maintenance tenant, the same way
truckers are lumber, cement is a fluid version
of concrete, black is gray and up is down

in a way a street is wide as the word, the
same way my shirt looks better with these stains,
or a window seems bigger when empty,
in the way a fatal blunder brings relief, a list
is a diverting narrative, and clouds are flags
and waves are arrows—a way past malice,
hope or sensation—the way a lobster is a giant,
pugilistic shrimp, a beehive means industry,

an anthill connotes destruction, and Mae
West is synonymous with the Old West.
A raindrop is a harbinger of asphyxia in much
the same way a tear loves a pressure drop,
Stewart Granger is an antonym for Texas Ranger,
a centipede connotes mathematical intrigue,
and one way usually means "no way"—
a way no circle tires of repeating

A COMPLEX ANSWER

A complex answer locked
the networks in a star-search for a sequel.
Sponsor breaks grew few and far between.
What was left on the air
broke into tiny moaning particles.

There were no bidding wars to monitor.
All footage mimed the flight patterns of bees.
Children found objects harder to swallow.
Women bled from inexplicable new places.

Men and power tools stumbled
blindly toward a suffocating silence,
evening folded, fell asleep under a chair—
all of it recounted later for the fanzines:

"Monday evening: the cries from
the cellar are shrill and heartbreaking.
Tuesday morning: an unnerving,
unscheduled solitude."

THREE SONGS

Progress

grammar is green
lovely is red
monkeys drive bargains
invention is dead

blues for the jailor
bile is the spread
diction apes splendour
inhales the instead

fend for the tender
spring for the bed
envy is golden
irony's threat

Detainee

I was questioned for bartering with beggars
arrested for squandering winter silence
accused of fleecing skittish sheep
detained for breaking wind successfully

I was questioned on a sudden turn of weather
arrested by an ant, mighty for its size
accused of exaggerating a sunrise
detained for fingering the moon

I was questioned for cutting a river's current
arrested for slackening a man's memory
accused of shimmering without a permit
detained for stains on my conscience

Piano Gag

the grapes of wrath decant
the leaves of grass derange
the wines of spring declaim
the branch of yew deplanes

every malice has its window
every kraken has its wake
every tipster plays the scoundrel
every dullard takes his cake

is it a matter of redress
that makes me so digress?
does a blunder torn asunder send
me thundering toward a sauna?

gag the piano and bait the snare
love is cruel and life unfair

ANTONIA IS NOT THE PLASTERER

I
Agnes, Betsy, Cornelius and Dexter each voted for a class president.
Dana is the cousin of the girl who attends Lincoln.
Pat studied the spelling list with Mickey and the other girl, but both did better in the contest than he did.
Lauren is a female, and the other two animals are male.

2.
Five students in each class (Bob, Cathy, Dan, Ed, Faye) are each the best at a certain subject.
Jorgenson used to work at Giant Corp. but then got a better offer from the company where she's working now.
The animal in the Tacoma Zoo, which is not the aardvark, can climb trees.
Ingram is younger than Lathem.

3.
Antonia, Colleen, Emmanuel and Gustav, whose last names are Dewey, Hamilton, Kennedy and Shaw, are a biologist, a flight attendant, a magician and a plasterer.
The person who voted for Hough is taller than Betsy and the person who voted for Grant.
The girl who attends Carver used to live next door to a boy named Nelson.
Jackie did better in the contest than Mickey did.

4.

Amherst, Bartlett, Croft, Davies and Enders each listened to a rebroadcast of an old radio program (*Fibber McGee and Molly, The Green Hornet, Jack Benny, The Lone Ranger, The Shadow*).

Lauren is larger than the animal who lives in the house.

Cathy and the student who is the best at handwriting had lunch at school with Bob and the student who is best at geography.

Litton, who has been with the same company for twenty years, worked her way up from the bottom.

5.

Five animals (aardvark, bear, cheetah, elephant, zebra) live in zoos in different cities (Detroit, Houston, Omaha, San Diego, Tacoma).

Debbie is younger than Harold but older than King and Art.

Shaw, who is not Antonia, is very good at her work, which is not part of the building industry.

Agnes did not vote for Hough.

6.

Dana, Ephram, John and Martha attend four different schools (Adams, Carver, King, Lincoln).

Pat studied the spelling list with Mickey and the other girl, but both did better in the contest than he did.

Enders didn't listen to the *Jack Benny* program.

The animal who lives in the barn is angry at the mouse who tricked him yesterday.

7.

Art, Bob, Cathy, Debbie and Harold have last names of Green, Ingram, Jones, King and Lathem.

The president of Big Co. and his wife go golfing several times a year.

The fastest animal is in the San Diego zoo.

Neither Amherst nor Croft listened to a comedy program.

8.

Bobby, Jackie, Mickey and Pat finished in first, second, third and fourth places in a spelling contest.

Bartlett listened to a program about the Old West.

Lauren is larger than the animal who lives in the house.

Dan and the student who is best at handwriting walked home from the school with the student who is best at reading.

9.

Figure out who (Jorgenson, Kiley, Litton, Tyler) is the president of which company (Big Co., Giant Corp., Mammoth Co., Super Co.).

The striped animal is not in a zoo in the southern part of the country.

Jones is older than either of the other men, but is younger than Green.

Kennedy, who is not the magician, is older than Hamilton and is younger than Emmanuel.

10.

Lauren, Norman and Peter are a cat, a dog and a mouse. They live in a barn, a garage and a house.

Dan, Cathy and the student who is best at spelling walked to school with Ed and the student who is best at geography.

The president of Big Co. and his wife go golfing several times a year.

Antonia is not the plasterer.

11.

Match them up from the clues below.

Match up the student and the subject from the clues below.

Match up everything from the clues below.

Match them up from the clues below.

Match up each animal with the zoo where it lives.

Match each person with the school attended.

Match the first names with the last names.
Figure out how each person did in the contest
and whether the person is a boy or a girl.
Kiley doesn't know the president of Mammoth Co. but has heard of him.
Figure out who is what and who lives where.

THREE SONNETS (ASSEMBLY REQUIRED)

aerodrome

melodrama

diphthong

dandruff

rhizome

dipstick

genome

phoneme

crudités

rhombus

dendrite

oblong

nimbus

syndrome

COUNTERPANE

Hello, lady people! Pigeons are good.
Winter is good. Stoolpigeons are good—
though they're in league with the government,
trying to kill all spontaneity.
Hello everyone! Time to start losing.
Losing is good. Losing is what we came
here to do, and it's going quite well,
thanks for asking.

This morning I was passed by a minivan,
"Someday" printed on the vanity plate.
I wonder what she meant? "Someday soon,
goin' with you" or "I'm gonna get out of
here someday?" or "Someday my prince,
or a real rain's going to come."

Given the words in advance, it
might all be easier. Interpretation—
that's where the problems start.
Take *counterpane*, for an example.
Sounds like a magician's con,
a glass counter you'd bounce coins
off, but really it means something
comforting—a blanket to keep you warm.

Coins bounce off the counterpane
and under that blanket, where they exist
now in the mind only, and so will multiply

at my request. Nothing too greedy,
enough for coffee and a newspaper,
somewhere I can look for a job, anything
to reverse the recent downturn.

People like people who stand for things.
Like Shakespeare arrived at Ellis Island with
a trussed-up suitcase and the equivalent of
$3.50 in badly out-of-date currency.
And look where he ended up.
A real job — I'd like that.
People like people who have jobs.
People like people who stand for things.

GALLERY

Winter

streets smother
ice is removed

cold lake sleeps at one end
streetcar thunders at the other

night: a throat of milk
stars: noose of old stone

Atheist Prayer

If man is god's image,
heaven is manmade.

I'd rather hang here.

The Gallery

opposite of a brothel
light oppressive
goods sequestered

security thick and
inattentive

WINSLOW, HOMER

1.
to wander a cacophony with the north wind as stoolpigeon
is to draw silence from a well kick it in the scrotum then
   pronounce it unfit to drive

2.
to scale Everest towing a plastic Zellers baby stroller
is to strand the sun permanently in a socket
   tedious to the elderly

3.
to erect a courthouse of baseballs and forcemeats
is to coax democracy toward a final euphony
   the flies all shagging the dogs

FATHERLY

1) *Mnemonic*

when the mites go up
the tites come down

2) *Cautionary*

shocking shocking shocking
the mouse ran up the stocking
when he got to the knee what did he see?
shocking shocking shocking

3) *Elegiac*

it's not the cough that carries you off
it's the coffin they carry you off in

LITANY

Were the doves disciplined according to the bylaws?

Yes.

Were their wings hacked off and thrown into the angry waters?

Yes.

Did they duck and quail at their predicament?

No.

Did their tiny throats emit anything resembling a pun?

No.

So they took their punishment honourably?

I'd say so. As much as they knew what was happening.

Stoically?

I wouldn't go that far.

Did the moon weep and fret at their growing peril?

Yes.

Did you weep?

No, not initially.

But when it came, did your weeping fill a thousand barrels?

Yes, and ten times as many.

When your tears came, did they fill a thousand thimbles?

No, not so much as that.

Did the beach ache with your misplaced sympathy?

No.

Can you think of a more apt metaphor for your distress?

Perhaps, but not at the moment.

Back to the beach—did the limpets slip, then attach themselves again?

No…I mean…no, I wasn't paying attention.

But did the gulls seem mostly undisturbed?

I couldn't say.

I'm sorry—it is your testimony that the gulls were disturbed or undisturbed?

I wasn't watching, my eyes were filled with tears.

In your opinion, was their interrogation entirely necessary?

Yes.

Considering the loss of life?

Yes.

In your own words: was the whole session conducted humanely?

No.

But, surely, you couldn't call it cruelly gratuitous?

I'd have to say...no.

Do you have a problem with how we handle such matters?

No...I mean, no.

You're very sure you're not holding something back?

No.

You do realize that would be foolish...and unnecessary.

[Unresponsive]

Are you holding something back?

Yes.

Would you be more comfortable with counsel present?

Yes.

So you explicitly request that we produce counsel?

No.

To be clear, you're still willing to continue with these questions?

[Unresponsive]

Have you been harboring doubts for long?

Doubts?

Your feelings of resentment toward our institutions?

No, not so very long.

Is that why you put on these ridiculous disguises?

No.

Is that why you've told all these obvious lies?

Sir. I've answered truthfully at all times.

Is there anything you'd like to say in your defense?

Only that these proceedings are a farce.

Is there anything you'd like to say in your defense?

Only that these proceedings are entirely justified.

Is there anything you'd like to say in your *defense?*

Only that the gulls were guiltless, however it may have looked.

Is there anything else you'd like to say before sentencing?

No.

Is there something you might like to say before sentencing...

That I'm sorry.

...before you're taken from this room, forever?

No. That is...yes. Only that I'm very, very sorry.

REWIND

a long night of sweating
a move toward something better
a malodorous towel
a wound to the forehead
a shared worry over a friend's poor behaviour
a dispute over time and money
a death, a developing illness
a dire prognosis
a holiday postponed
a sense of storming out
a firing, common cause lost,
a loyalty tested
a decision to work within unacceptable limits
a period of confusion
a realization of promise
a time of great prospects
a meeting of friends beside a lake
a good turn
an intense period of emptiness
a feeling of loss and disillusion
a friendship betrayed
a period of restlessness
a sense of useful work and promise
a deepening of feeling
a sense of being tested
a sense of life going much better than expected
a whirlwind courtship
a sense of giddy weightlessness

a feeling of being locked out
a drunken wandering after dark
a catacomb escaped
an understanding that we must never tell the truth
a period of constant apology
a flurry of youthful transgression
a sudden understanding that knowing solves nothing
a stain on a car seat
a collision with other lives, often at random
an intense frustration with stasis
a glorious torpor
an unwarranted sense of importance
a funny white hat
a photograph on school premises
a role in a play, rehearsed, turned down
a growth spurt
a feeling of being small for your age
a new image
a stagy walk in the rain
an encounter with problems not your own
and far too large for you
a prize won, a love unspoken
a love spurned, a love imagined
a sense of something larger always looming
a rummage sale
a friend with a pool table
a punch missed and a punch taken
a friend fleeing over the lawn
a small yard huge with possibilities
a tin of dead tadpoles
a field, a net

a room with a laundry chute
a dimly witnessed drive cross-country
a reprimand
a yard filled with broken glass
father swearing, hitting his head
a fever, a snoring vaporizer
woman's shape in the doorway
a caress
a shadow over the bed humming
a wet warmth, an eruption:
violent thunder above

CLEAN HEAD
for Daniel Jones

To you it's a pincer, to the crab
it's just the crutch that keeps him up
nights, upright in a sudden current,
or the force that backs him into

the metaphor of a very famous poet,
or the thing that gets him boiled
and quartered over drawn butter.
Like tattooing and piercing is cool,

but if I pulled a knife, ran it over my face
diagonally, maybe nicked an eye
or something—because I thought I'd
look dead windswept—everyone who

knows me would fear for my sanity.
An ominous sign, they'd say, like
a radical change in hairstyle, a
cry for help favoured by the suicidal.

And it's true—the one friend I know
who killed himself died with a clean
head and a fresh prescription.
But illness is not the sum of it. Not really.

Really it's about still caring—about
what duels you, scares you to death.
Seconds tumbled smooth like stones.
Nauseous flyboy stumbling to the tarmac,

as if the sudden quiet, this sense of being
grounded, was all new to him.

NEVER NOW

What convinces soon evaporates, ditches,
sets out on junkets you allowed time for,
though it tests the professional feathers.

You'd see New Zealand at least, as an
adult, if that makes a difference, and just
maybe it does, though it has no long-term

repercussions: now is never now, not even
in the way that forwards this small statement.
We get here via some more devious route:

Breathe in, breathe out, that's what it's all about.
So we're told and so we believe and so we
surrender to it. But passion in the head is

not passion in the knees, as you well know.
It's as if we never thought about *it*, we were
so busy thinking it would all be about *later*...

and, yes, yes, of course it was...

POWDER KEG

The violins declare
my death wish uninteresting.
"Where's the hook?" they fret,
"the retribution, the Jill Ireland?"

They have a point,
and a whole string of puns I've
resisted exploiting, so you can
stop already with the bitching…

These can't be rational, can they?
Suspicions I'm dead already,
heart a basketball rasping obscenities
through a needled poohole?

Kennedy demanded purity,
refused the bubble overcover,
met his public and his maker
in the same driven show.

Let's decide now, it's all a euphemism:
"I hang my hammer by the claw
in your dewy branches…." Which
could mean anything, granted,

but you'd have to agree
it's pretty suggestive.
Like the grass that grows
under your feet and over mine.

DO DALLAS

Conspiracy? Sure.
But he posed it.
He ordered it.
Forget the dodgy shadows.

Your doubt. Your iconography.
Yours truly, we don't want it anymore.

Maybe there were two of them,
three of them, everyone who was there.
From those who ducked to those who
ran a quiet camera over it.

But only those who've seen it
can't see it for what it is.
Simple. Lucky. Bang.

LIKE SANTA

Cheese was made with real cheese
lawn was fed real grass
The forest was built on real wood
stars fired with real fire

Mosquitoes ran on real blood
doors planed over vintage knots
Windows filled with real skies
the tires were all tired

Hearts really had a heart
petals worked on genuine pedals
The sun was good-natured much of the time
joy busted in like Santa

but the cobbles were stoned
and the worms ran like stockings
It really was the cough that carried you off—
dawn tipped her hat of shadows

NO WINDOWS

they look for a white van they look for the man who killed the girl
a van with no windows filled with candy the man was in the van but
he is not there now the journalist is very sorry they look for a man
who is at large and not represented accurately in this drawing of a van
with no windows drawn by a nine-year-old boy the man they look
for was in the van that went down the boy's street many times but the
boy did not make the picture until he knew the man who took the
girl was the same man who offered to drive him and his sister to
McDonald's then ran home to tell his mother they look for the man
any trace of him or the van or the candy which he may have used to
take the girl the journalist has pictures of the girl he shows on TV
but in those pictures the girl has not been taken yet the boy knows
they'll never find the man with these pictures because the girl who
in those pictures was alive is now dead and the pictures of the man's
van are inaccurate though excellent for a boy of nine if you look at
his rough picture and picture a van in your mind or even picture a
more accurate drawing of a white van with no windows it might be
amazingly close to the van known to be driven by the man they now
look for there are people in the driveway of the girl's house who want
to talk to the father of the girl in the pictures who is now dead though
you can't tell it from these pictures in which she looks quite happy
while the journalist is very sad a drawing of a van drives down the
street of the sad girl who is now tragically dead and inside the
drawing is a drawing of a man who looks different from the police
suspect in the picture taken before the girl was now tragically dead
a van with no windows stops it picks up a picture of the girl they
were looking for but stopped looking for because she has now been
confirmed dead in the picture she looks full of life everyone on the
TV is crying the journalist kisses her grandmother on the forehead
everyone is crying no one can believe it

INJURY

No different from any other telling insult:
you want no part of it at first, resist any
and all signs it even exists, and when it's
undeniable, fabricate a self-defined remedy
—talk your way out, throw some ice on it,
push the splintered balsa back together...

If it can be walked on, it can't be screwed,
and so your self-serving routine can't be broken,
though you're also keen for a break from that
trap, which you know you're allowing, slowly
and without a registered vote, to kill you—
like butter or extreme sports or melanoma.

So fall off the karaoke chair, Jenny, drunk and
gorgeous, stumble around Tokyo wingless for days.
Take a little industrial shrapnel in the chest, Michael,
watch vainly for its slow promised rebirth.
Expose that long rail of stitches, Matthew, it'll add
a little bite to your quick unconscious kindness,

which only an idiot can't see as edge enough.
What lives over bone is fragile, doomed really.
These hurts and the deals we broker with them—
bad, good, disastrous—outlive any improv...
however diverting, however smitten
with the underrated glamour of being.

REVOLVER

A tiny acrobat walks a rope of milk;
whitewash in microform, history pelted
by the poop of our teens. Mudslide, cataclysm,
events of weather to be surfed if possible,
thought through carefully when necessary—
what turns slowly turns hard against you

and no question, it always turns. Consequence?
Sure. But who lives for that moment?—missed
course, quick panic, the drunk cousin left behind
heaving and spitting up. Look him in the eye—
watch the cones swell, thrill the estuaries.
Buckwheat's line: "Isthmus be my lucky day."

And isn't it always lucky days—
revolver, revolver, noon and moon, midnight.

IV

SUNDIAL

You drop into conversation like an
afternoon dives into an empty swimming
pool—gamely but down an element.

It's a fall day and a short week,
the streetcar's cavern backlit with heads
and arms: a turkey shoot, a roach motel.

You say you feel qualified to talk
about the service here, having served up
so many slices of yourself over the years.

You've grown weak from bowling olives
at free radicals and chained pit bulls—
their days (both of them) are numbered.

I have my rant about transience and intransigence.
You like to run down the simile as a viable
artistic strategy—you call it "sex through

a sheet," but the way you call it that
makes it so vividly sexy: the sheet
with my name on it, the sad euphemism

lugeing its way toward the gap,
downspout, spinning into unknown.
I was told this was how they vote in Japan,

but I'm not sure I believe a word of it
anymore: that raft of rabble and nogoodniks,
their avowed allegiance to the way things stand.

And so we scroll through the hours, like the
fireball scours the skin of a bank tower:
tireless rehearsal of the dark scenes in tow.

AUNT OLIVE AMONGST THE HEAVY-PETTERS

When she's not talking, and that's rare enough even with the
goiter, she can't hear a thing—a plus for an old girl who,
unlike her kin, ends one bottle before opening another.
There's glass plastered into garden walls, a threat of poison
tossed in with the carp and lettuce and marine lilies.
Throw as many googlies as you like—there's no one to lob
your balls back, not like at Normandy, not like the B of B.
There's Herbert, rangy brother, rung twitchy by the Blitz and
fled for Spain; sister Doris trapped by jealousy and duty
and bingo; two sons and their brood of boys—too
young and squirmy to kiss you properly,

though you remember the pier as it was, before the moribund
casino and manmade "recreation" pond, crowds so big then
young lovers risked the low tide for a bit of privacy.
Salt on a lip's kiss, little hands shoved up under your jumper.
Who could resist their boldness, who'd want to? The rejected
and leftover, sunlit cads, and best—the hungry boys,
dead and buried in their minds already, improbably reprieved.

PULL

through haze, under this sky, tectonic gathering of buildings
in deep grass, light panting under a yellow umbrella
a face opens and retreats, opens, opens again, regroups, stays open
telltale gesture, truant but familiar, played over lips before bed
the difference between me and you is I'm not affected
you collide with darkness, never sure what set it spinning

in deep grass, light panting under a yellow umbrella
through haze, under this sky, tectonic gathering of buildings
you collide with darkness, never sure what set it spinning
telltale gesture, truant but familiar, played over lips before bed
the difference between me and you is I'm unaffected
a face opens and retreats, opens, opens again, regroups, stays open

in deep grass, light panting under a yellow umbrella
telltale gesture, truant but familiar, played over lips before bed
the difference between me and you is I'm not afflicted
you collide with darkness, never sure what set it spinning
through haze, under this sky, tectonic gathering of buildings
a face opens and retreats, opens, opens again, regroups, stays open

the difference between me and you is I'm not on fire
you collide with darkness, never sure what set it spinning
telltale gesture, truant but familiar, played over lips before bed
in deep grass, light panting under a yellow umbrella
a face opens and retreats, opens, opens again, regroups, stays open
through haze, under this sky, tectonic gathering of buildings

a face opens and retreats, opens, opens again, regroups, stays open
you collide with darkness, never sure what set it spinning
through haze, under this sky, tectonic gathering of buildings
telltale gesture, truant but familiar, played over lips before bed
in deep grass, light panting under a yellow umbrella
the difference between me and you is I'm not conflicted

a face opens and retreats, opens, opens again, regroups, stays open
through haze, under this sky, tectonic gathering of buildings
telltale gesture, truant but familiar, played over lips before bed
the difference between me and you is I'm not sorry
you collide with darkness, never sure what set it spinning
in deep grass, light panting under a yellow umbrella

THIRTY-ONE

Your skin is pierced with hunted hearts
I trifled with and left for lost.
Their full wings, airy arts?
Frail instruments I took for ghosts.

How many trawled and bleachy drips
have strangled on those fingertips?
Ditties for the dead, speaking parts,
which now seem less-than-pretty trips

downriver, where they peddle frowns.
Past grasses any current drowns,
you followed every line I tossed
with swallows only you could dodge.

All skin I took, I swallow freely now,
and you (all heart) scale every rib of me.

STANDARD

My funny time after time
hear me say that I'm
so lucky to be the one you run
to see someone to watch
over the many charms about
you sometimes wonder why
they're writing arms about you
my memory of love

[refrain]

was a fall to get that way
fool to sigh alas a loss
a lucky day although
you can't dismiss a memory
a kiss but not for me one look
at you laughable irreplaceable
unphotographable

[refrain]

coo you can but could
you care above all I want
your heart tipsy less than gipsy
your figure Greek a little weak
just one look at you pardons
my mush my funny world
you each day being Valentine's

ORENTHALOGY

Our royal escapee, not Martin Luther, not even Rodney:
Rex populi, our favourite unhung unsung hero.
Even the garbage couldn't sell you out,
Notwithstanding the outstanding remains—
The wife without a throat, waiter without a life and
How's that whole meal sitting, now we've brought it up?

All night some nights—many, I'd guess—
Late into it. Though we're better at it now:
Just play it like its chalked, as trained.
Some talk big and others fucking deliver:

It's something you don't want, send it back; it
Mocks you, take it out; put it through its
Paces, but, yeah then, *boom!*, out with the trash.
So we know you did it, and so what?
On any given day, it's still libel…though
Not actionable, or we'd all be in the shit.

FISH

You crossed the bride with the fish in your hat,
passed under her stars breathless, unimpressed.
Autumn is an impresario, winter, the drop dead,
these are lessons we can neither follow nor bed,
skipping classes, warnings, footprints on the bread

I've been coasting on sequins and cliff-dives
their dullard landings, vainglorious concubines
Lilt of tossed awnings: pleasant once—witty
sometimes, even—but so grim now they're useless:
no solvent sets that feathered sort free

Half-drunk, half-interested, arrested half-asleep,
up-to-something…maybe/must-be…in the gap,
malaise, interstice, elapse. A trigger or a moan,
synapse, asp or adze. The hook of it that pitted,
vexed, gassed: a gilled oar open to suggestion

LOVE SONG

Desire is the supreme beautician
  —A.R. AMMONS

She was disgusted by the way he sweated,
sometimes for no reason, sometimes not at all

by his flatulence, which could arrive
at any time and which he played for cute

She was disgusted by his broken teeth, which he
brushed incessantly, like a dog after a bone

by his belly, which hung about him like
bags of dirty water

She was disgusted by his dull scent, stronger
the more he tried to hide it

by his way of talking over her, the courtly
way he let her finish

She was disgusted by the hair on his back,
his moles, the crud that built up in his nose

by his bluff toughness, neediness,
his knack for turning everything to his advantage

She was disgusted by his desperation, the
way he seemed to die right before her eyes

by his lousy timing and false bravado,
the way he'd allow her room to breathe

on the one day she craved closeness.
She was disgusted by his sensitivity…the gall of it…

Still, she had to have him, and that was that

CYCLE

The sound of rain annihilating itself on the grass
outside this window, which holds a sleeping cat,
is so pleasant it seems like unrepentant pandering,

like the underslung tumble of night cloud that
predicted it, stage whisper in the evening leaves
that preceded that, or a late afternoon that

always shapes up better than expected, midday
birds who lurch theatrically, only shit on the
lucky, scraps of breakfast you threw to one

in particular, who's always pushed aside;
and the morning struggle that led up to it:
headache and coffee, startled wakening from

a baffled, exhausting dream in wrung-out sheets,
too-warm presence of your sleeping honey instantly
calming, eyes wandering lids, lips in quarter-smile,

breath day-old, fermented, but still wildly pleasant,
her face childlike and frankly, beautiful—no other word
works—open as she is to all pains and every window.

SKIES

These skies unchanging,
inexcusable, irreversible, no care
nor hope nor pity moves them—
such is the thoughtful duty of skies

We deserve better, less doubtable,
more constant; cares little of your
wants, your craven motions—
such is the thoughtless beauty of skies

When they race they cut like stones,
still skies crave torsion, even strength:
leave smarts to those other worlds—
such is the careless pity of skies

GOOD NEWS BAD

the way
rain on 3 a.m. wind
drives
like an overdue taxi

pushes you
out onto the porch
in worry or hope
you can never decide

which is still a better
place, better use
of what you were
struggling with

the way
it gasps and settles,
dashes, retreats —
brings everything to light

LAST ONE ON THE MOON

How could something so rote,
so written, find time to surprise?
Niche of cliché, nemesis of fresh,
yet there it is again, lording it over the
firing dust, silhouettes of trees…
Never agreed to be extras, never think of
themselves as frames, never thought a thing
except in this drowsy context, which
morphs into heartfelt syntax, scares that
cynic heart you worship straight.

It's not that you want to stand up there
(you do), it's that it stands you up
in an uncomfortable cold that's always
cold now, on a bike, on a bike path
pressing down, beside a highway suddenly
tragic without its pointless imagined
lunar road signs…panting over
spinning wheels, which have never
in your experience struck you as ancient
or orbital, though they are now as
surely as they won't be tomorrow.

Perhaps it speaks to childhood: last one
on the moon's a rotten egg, lost morning,
poor reflection of what happened here
just twenty-one seconds ago, right here beside
you, and bounced back. Wrong? Sure.
Terracentrically incorrect. Any light in that
gray eye could only be the fireball itself.

Except for us, concerned with all those things
thinking wastes: hacks and demons, the
drowned and the saved, glad dogs still
digging all these deep hours into night.

THE PLAY
after Charles Simic

About a summer
which is too cold
to be summer

About its moaning
old undertow
which doesn't help

About its fear of
intimacy which holds
firm notwithstanding

Its marinated raw fish
which purists call
ceviche

Its blood
which is dubious
and equally imaginary

The art of sounding
its keening colours
as they stray—

racket-stringing
with the cat
as bait

How I drank to
its end in a
dream of minks

DOUBLE SUICIDE

However fondly devised, there's something feral
about it: that identical strangers would want out
in the exact increment it takes to push past reason,
that one wouldn't love it more than another, his fix
on her the narcotic that makes her miss her stop.

Of course, it's a matter of assumption—your lover
wouldn't let it go, but surely Christ or somesuch might
—it not really *your* idea, him that hopeless about the lost
job, lost hope, lost baby, lost chance to fix Dad
finally, for what he did or didn't do.

Photos being photos, they record the watcher's tones.
No soliloquy outthinks its author. Still, the camera
captures blinds, bodies, bed, and the swallowed logic:
destroy her as she'd destroyed him, or surely would
have, faced with the sight of her dead.

I REALLY NEED TED LILLY TO THROW THE HOOK

We're up two and I'm sick to death of losing.
It's Posada, never an easy out, but the hook
is there for Lilly. It's the seventh and his old team,
the 250-million-dollar Yankees, have beaten the
shit out of us all week. Faced with a real
pitcher, they're driving up the count,
knowing its Speier or Ligtenberg or Frasor
to follow, who never seem to get a call, or
forgot how to pitch the minute they put on the
stupid new uniform. High fastball…strike. Change,
down the shoot, whiff. Fastball, fishing, off the plate.

And now I really need Ted Lilly to throw the hook.
It changes nothing, but it's suddenly important now.

LIKE GOATS OR FLOWERS,

like reeds, even swimmers
gawk at stones in rivers, waste
their breath, lunch money,
prospects with a lover, bright
gasps less alluring than
some daft argument
against a sure thing.

This is not it, the stone says.
Not done. *Here a while yet.*
Might even scare back an instant,
chase a breath if you're clever,
something saved to sip on later.

An experiment: watch light
catch a current's muscle, one swell
stumbling, clearing the instrument,
then get your face down low, where
water boulders and crowns, slides
through. Now what do you see?

Constant birth or endless passage?
So why linger on stone? Because
it appears constant, or because you know
it's only here that you can carve a pause,
fingers pressed against current,
wrist, never conceding for an instant

that a moment—a breath even—
this one for instance, ends.

MAGIC LIGHT,

the one filmmakers dote on
coming in late and long

under a bright sheet of cloud
makes us suddenly bearable

and the (plain ugly) yellow
farmhouse seem even vain

because of the heat
pushed through small windows

toward back rooms
back porch backyard

where there's a shed maybe
(a dog), wading pool, car

someone loved enough to
hang on to far past reason

And is it so wrong to want
(so terrible to love?)

the larval imperative: bald makes
butterfly, fur means moth

PLENTY

The sky, lit up like a question or
an applause meter, is beautiful
like everything else today: the leaves
in the gutters, salt stains on shoes,
the girl at the IGA who looks just like
Julie Delpy, but you don't tell her—
she's too young to get the reference and
coming from you it'll just seem creepy.
So much beauty today you can't find
room for it, closets already filled
with beautiful trees and smells and
glances and clever turns of phrase.
Behind the sky there's a storm
on the way, which, with your luck,
will be a beautiful storm—dark
clouds beautiful as they arguably are,
the rain beautiful as it always is—
even lightning can be beautiful in a
scary kind of way (there's a word
for that, but let's forget it for the moment).
And maybe the sun will hang in long
enough to light up a few raindrops—
like jewels or glass or those bright beads
girls put between the letters on the
bracelets that spell out their beautiful names—
Skye or Miranda or Verandah—which isn't
even a name, although it is a word
we use to call things what they are,
and would be a pleasant place to sit
and watch the beautiful sky, beautiful

storm, the people with their beautiful
names walking toward the lake
in lovely clothing saying unpleasant
things over the phone about the people
they work with, all of it just adding to the
mother lode, the *surfeit* of beauty,
which on this day is just a fancy way
of saying lots, too much, skidloads, plenty.

NOTES ON THE POEMS

Page 12: "June Bug" is composed entirely of Mark Twain aphorisms, cut up and rearranged.

Page 17: "A Complex Answer" is a gloss on Darrell Gray's poem, "A Simple Answer," from *Something Swims Out* (Blue Wind, 1972).

Page 20: "Antonia Is Not the Plasterer" collages text from Anita Harnadek's *Mind Benders: Deductive Thinking Skills* (Midwest Publications, 1981).

Page 28: "Winslow, Homer" is a gloss on Pete Winslow's poem ("For Schlecter Duvall") in *Daisy in the Memory of a Shark* (City Lights, Pocket Poets Series 31, 1973).

Page 30: "Litany" was inspired by Michael Benedikt's poem of the same name, from his collection, *The Body* (Wesleyan, 1969).

Page 48: The first line of "Revolver" (and the inspiration for the title) are from poems in Pete Winslow's *Daisy in the Memory of a Shark* (City Lights, Pocket Poets Series 31, 1973).

Page 54: One line from "Pull" (the one that changes from stanza to stanza) is borrowed from *The Difference between Me and You Is That I'm Not on Fire* (Too Pure, 2004), the final album from Cardiff alt-rock trio Mclusky.

Page 56: "Thirty-One" is a gloss on William Shakespeare's Sonnet 31.

ACKNOWLEDGEMENTS

Some of these poems have appeared, or will appear (often in slightly different form), in the following publications:

"Last One on the Moon" in *Maisonneuve*
"Cycle" in *The Walrus*
"No Windows," "Double Suicide," and "Winter" in *dig*
"Sundial" in *This Magazine*
"Plenty" in *Taddle Creek*
"Piano Gag," "Detainee," and "Winslow, Homer" in the anthology *Surreal Estate: 13 Canadian Poets Under the Influence* (Mercury Press, 2004).

Many thanks to the respective editors.

The first drafts of "Audition Piece" and "Counterpane" were written in ten minutes as part of the Silent Slam at Toronto's Drake Hotel, April 7, 2005, and were later published in a chapbook documenting the event. Thanks to the organizers and especially Sandra Alland for cajoling me into participating.

"Pull" was written to accompany a short film by Toronto artist Darya Farha in the inaugural Poetry/Projections collaboration project in 2005. Thanks to her, to L.I.F.T., and to Richard Vaughan for getting me involved.

Thanks to Damian Rogers and the folks at Wave Books in the U.S. for including me in the Canadian leg of their Poetry Bus odyssey (www.poetrybus.com) in 2006, a uniquely positive experience for me and many others.

Finally, thanks to Gil Adamson for her smarts and indispensable encouragement; to my friend and editor Ken Babstock (who has a very polite way of insisting); to Bill Douglas for the cover design and Eamon Mac Mahon for the cover photograph; and to Laura, Lynn, Sarah, Matt, and the rest of the gang at Anansi for sticking up for poets.

This book was hugely assisted by a grant from the Canada Council for the Arts and several smaller grants from the Ontario Arts Council through its Writer's Reserve Program.

ABOUT THE AUTHOR

Kevin Connolly is a poet, journalist and editor. He has published three previous collections of poetry, most recently *drift* (Anansi, 2005), which won the Trillium Poetry Award. He lives on a cat farm in Toronto's east end with his partner, writer Gil Adamson.